# Humpty Dumpty

Music engraved by Note-orious Productions Limited.
Illustrations by Lee Nicholls.

Order No. AM 975590
US International Standard Book Number: 0.8256.2762.1
UK International Standard Book Number: 0.7119.9682.2

Exclusive Distributors:
**Music Sales Corporation**
257 Park Avenue South, New York, NY 10010 USA
**Music Sales Limited**
8/9 Frith Street, London W1D 3JB England
**Music Sales Pty. Limited**
120 Rothschild Street, Rosebery, Sydney, NSW 2018, Australia

Printed in the United States of America by
Vicks Lithograph and Printing Corporation

**Amsco Publications**
*New York/London/Paris/Sydney/Copenhagen/Berlin/Tokyo/Madrid*

# CD track listing

1. Humpty Dumpty
2. Grand Old Duke Of York
3. Jack And Jill
4. I'm A Little Teapot
5. Bobby Shaftoe
6. Mary, Mary Quite Contrary
7. Michael Finnegan
8. This Old Man
9. Teddy Bear, Teddy Bear
10. Little Miss Muffet
11. Curly Locks
12. See Saw Margery Daw
13. Pat-A-Cake, Pat-A-Cake
14. Polly Put The Kettle On
15. Tommy Thumb
16. Have You Seen The Muffin Man?

# Contents

# Humpty Dumpty

## TRADITIONAL

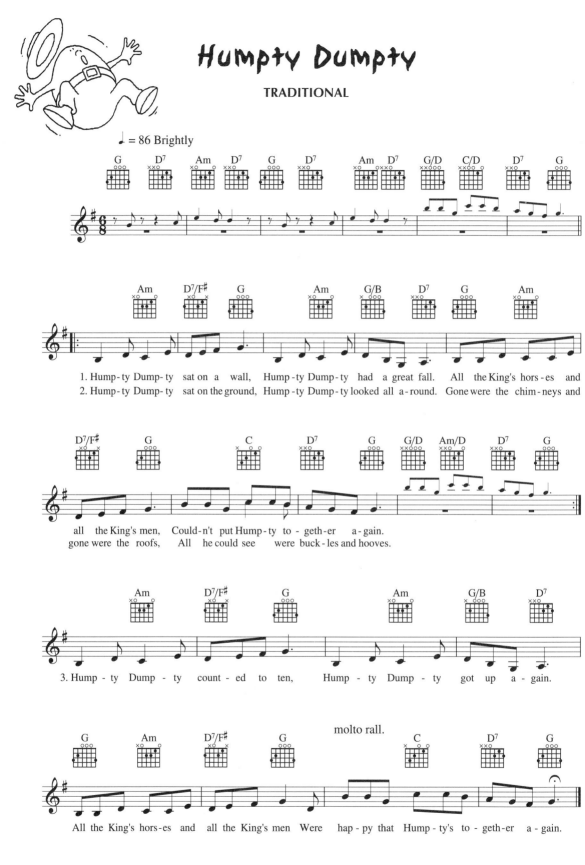

1. Hump-ty Dump-ty sat on a wall, Hump-ty Dump-ty had a great fall. All the King's hors-es and
2. Hump-ty Dump-ty sat on the ground, Hump-ty Dump-ty looked all a-round. Gone were the chim-neys and

all the King's men, Could-n't put Hump-ty to-geth-er a-gain.
gone were the roofs, All he could see were buck-les and hooves.

3. Hump-ty Dump-ty count-ed to ten, Hump-ty Dump-ty got up a-gain.

molto rall.

All the King's hors-es and all the King's men Were hap-py that Hump-ty's to-geth-er a-gain.

# Grand Old Duke Of York

## TRADITIONAL

♩ = 100 Military march

Oh, the Grand Old Duke of York, he had ten thou - sand men. He marched them up to the top of the hill and he marched them down a - gain. And when they were up they were up, and when they were down they were down, And when they were on - ly half - way up they were nei - ther up nor down. Oh, the

1.

2.

# Jack And Jill

## TRADITIONAL

♩. = 120 With a bounce!

Jack and Jill went up the hill to fetch a pail of wa - ter. Jack fell down and broke his crown, and Jill came tum - bl - ing af - ter. Up Jack got and home he trot as fast as he could ca - per, He went to bed, to mend his head with vi - ne - gar and brown pa - per.

# I'm A Little Teapot

**TRADITIONAL**

**Verse 2:**

I'm a tube of toothpaste on the shelf,
I get so lonely all by myself.
When it gets to night time then I shout,
Just lift my lid off, squeeze me out!
Lift my lid off, squeeze me out!

**Verse 3:**

I'm a little teapot, short and stout.
Here's my handle, here's my spout.
When I get all steamed up, hear me shout,
Tip me over, pour me out!
Tip me over, pour me out!

# Bobby Shaftoe

**TRADITIONAL**

Bob - by Shaf - toe's gone to sea, Sil - ver buck - les on his knee. He'll come back and mar - ry me,

1. Bon - nie Bob - by Shaf - toe. Bob - by Shaf - toe's tall and slim, Al - ways dressed so neat and trim. Las - ses they all smile at him, Bon - nie Bob - by Shaf - toe.

2.

Bob - by Shaf - toe's bright and fair, Comb - ing down his yel - low hair,

He's my love for ev - er - more, Bon - nie Bob - by Shaf - toe.

Bob - by Shaf - toe's gone to sea, Sil - ver buck - les on his knee.

He'll come back and mar - ry me, Bon - nie Bob - by Shaf - toe.

# Mary, Mary Quite Contrary

**TRADITIONAL**

Mar - y, Mar - y, quite con - trar - y, how does your gar - den grow? "With

sil - ver bells and cock - le shells and pret - ty maids all in a row."

Ma - ry, Ma - ry, quite con - tra - ry, how does your gar - den grow? "With

sil - ver bells and cock - le shells and pret - ty maids all in a row.

rit.

# Michael Finnegan

**TRADITIONAL**

Lively hillbilly ♩ = 110

1. There

was an old man called Mi-chael Fin-ne-gan, He grew whisk-ers on his chin-ne-gan. The
was an old man called Mi-chael Fin-ne-gan, He went fish-ing with a pin a-gain. He

wind came up and blew them in a-gain. Poor old Mi-chael Fin-ne-gan. Be-gin a-gain.
caught a fish then dropped it in a-gain! Poor old Mi-chael Fin-ne-gan. Be-gin a-gain.

1.

2. There

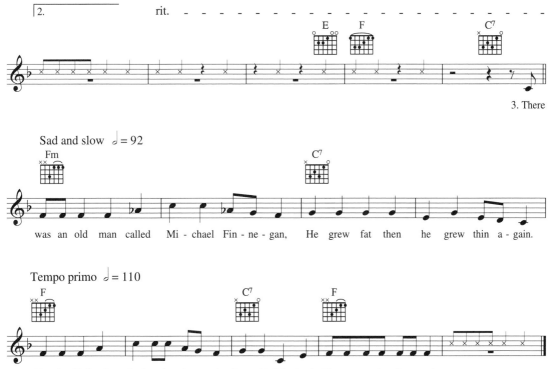

2.       rit. - - - - - - - - - - - - - - - - - - -

E    F          C⁷

3. There

**Sad and slow** ♩ = 92

Fm                       C⁷

was an old man called Mi - chael Fin - ne - gan, He grew fat then he grew thin a - gain.

**Tempo primo** ♩ = 110

F                      C⁷         F

Then he died and     had to be-gin a-gain, Poor old Mi-chael Fin-ne-gan be-gin a-gain

# This Old Man

## TRADITIONAL

Jolly ♩ = 104

1. This old man, he played one, He played nick - nack on my drum, With a nick - nack, pad - dy - wack,
2. This old man, he played two, He played nick - nack on my shoe, With a nick - nack, pad - dy - wack,

give a dog a bone. This old man came roll - ing home.
give a dog a bone. This old man came roll - ing home.

*Verse 3:*

This old man, he played three,
He played nick-nack on my knee,
*etc.*

*Verse 4:*

This old man, he played four,
He played nick-nack on my floor,
*etc.*

*Verse 5:*

This old man, he played five,
He played nick-nack on my hive,
*etc.*

*Verse 6:*

This old man, he played six,
He played nick-nack on my sticks,
*etc.*

*Verse 7:*

This old man, he played seven,
He played nick-nack up in heaven,
*etc.*

*Verse 8:*

This old man, he played eight,
He played nick-nack at my gate,
*etc.*

*Verse 9:*

This old man, he played nine,
He played nick-nack on my spine,
*etc.*

*Verse 10:*

This old man, he played ten,
He played nick-nack once again,
*etc.*

# Teddy Bear, Teddy Bear

**TRADITIONAL**

Like a lullaby ♩ = 96

1. Ted - dy Bear, Ted - dy Bear, turn a - round, ___ Ted - dy Bear, Ted - dy Bear, touch the ground.

Ted - dy Bear, Ted - dy bear, show your shoe, ___ Ted - dy Bear, Ted - dy Bear that will do.

Ted - dy Bear, Ted - dy Bear, say good night.

*Verse 2:*

Teddy Bear, Teddy Bear, climb the stairs,
Teddy Bear, Teddy Bear, say your prayers.
Teddy Bear, Teddy Bear, turn off the light,
Teddy Bear, Teddy Bear, say good night.

# Little Miss Muffet

## TRADITIONAL

Lit - tle Miss Muf - fet sat on her tuf - fet, eat - ing her curds and whey. There

came a big spi - der which sat down be - side her and fright - ened Miss Muf - fet a - way. And

fright - ened Miss Muf - fet a - way.

Lit - tle Miss Muf - fet sat on her tuf - fet, eat - ing her curds and whey. There

came a big spi - der which sat down be - side her and fright - ened Miss Muf - fet a -

rit.

way. And fright - ened Miss Muf - fet a - way.

# Curly Locks

**TRADITIONAL**

Gently ♪ = 132

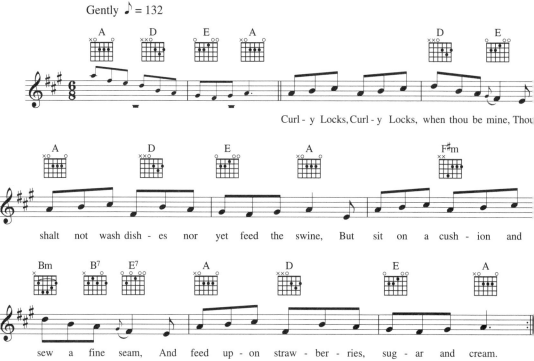

Curl - y Locks, Curl - y Locks, when thou be mine, Thou shalt not wash dish - es nor yet feed the swine, But sit on a cush - ion and sew a fine seam, And feed up - on straw - ber - ries, sug - ar and cream.

# See Saw Margery Daw

**TRADITIONAL**

Steadily ♩. = 69

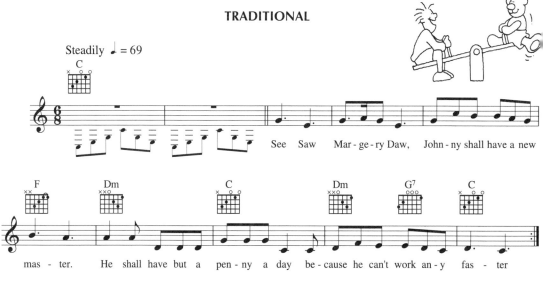

See Saw Mar - ge - ry Daw, John - ny shall have a new mas - ter. He shall have but a pen - ny a day be - cause he can't work an - y fas - ter

# Pat-A-Cake, Pat-A-Cake

**TRADITIONAL**

Slow one-in-a-bar feel ♩ = 44

Pat - a - cake, pat - a - cake bak - er's man. Bake me a cake____ as

fast as you can. Pat it and prick it and mark it with

*rit. (on repeat)*

'B', and put it in the ov - en for ba - by and me.

# Polly Put The Kettle On

**TRADITIONAL**

Pol - ly put the ket - tle on we'll all have tea.

Su - ki take it off a - gain, Su - ki take it off a - gain,

Su - ki take it off a - gain, they've all gone a - way!

Pol - ly put the ket - tle on, Pol - ly put the ket - tle on,

Pol - ly put the ket - tle on, we'll all have tea.

Su - ki take it off a - gain, Su - ki take it off a - gain,

Su - ki take it off a - gain, they've all gone a - way!

# Tommy Thumb

## TRADITIONAL

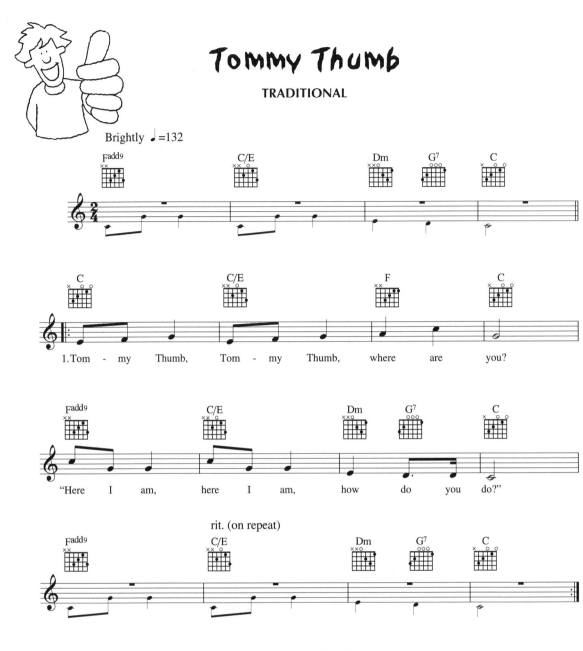

Brightly ♩=132

1.Tom - my Thumb, Tom - my Thumb, where are you?

"Here I am, here I am, how do you do?"

rit. (on repeat)

*Verse 2:*

Peter Pointer, Peter Pointer, where are you?
"Here I am, here I am, how do you do?"

*Verse 3:*

Middle Man, Middle Man, where are you?
"Here I am, here I am, how do you do?"

*Verse 4:*

Ruby Ring, Ruby Ring, where are you?
"Here I am, here I am, how do you do?"

*Verse 5:*

Baby Small, Baby Small, where are you?
"Here I am, here I am, how do you do?"

*Verse 6:*

Fingers all, fingers all, where are you?
"Here we are, here we are, how do you do?"

# Have You Seen The Muffin Man?

**TRADITIONAL**

yes, we've seen the Muf - fin Man, the Muf - fin Man, the Muf - fin Man. Oh

yes, we've seen the Muf - fin Man who lives down Dru – ry Lane.

*Verse 2:*

Oh, yes, I've seen the Muffin Man,
The Muffin Man, The Muffin Man.
Oh, yes, I've seen the Muffin Man
Who lives down Drury Lane.